Tanks

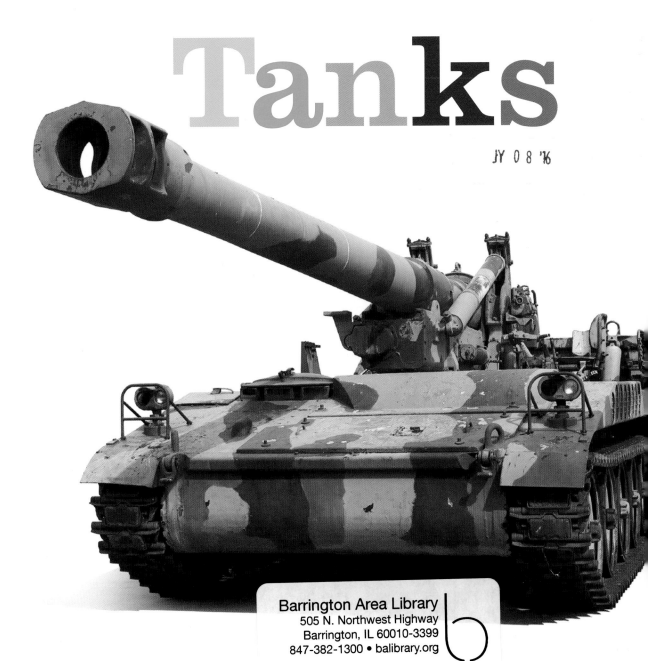

Laura K. Murray

CREATIVE EDUCATION • CREATIVE PAPERBACKS

seedlings

Published by Creative Education and Creative Paperbacks
P.O. Box 227, Mankato, Minnesota 56002
Creative Education and Creative Paperbacks
are imprints of The Creative Company
www.thecreativecompany.us

Design by Ellen Huber; production by Travis Green
Art direction by Rita Marshall
Printed in the United States of America

Photographs by Bigstock (Abidika), Corbis (Ed Darack/
Science Faction, Leif Skoogfors), DefenseImagery (Sgt.
Roberto Di Giovine), Dreamstime (Bigrock, Oleg Doroshin,
Elswarro, David Máška, Oleg Nesterkin, Daniel Raustadt,
Nico Smit, Stangot, Upimages), Getty Images, iStockphoto
(hipproductions, narvikk, RoyalFive), Shutterstock (ID1974,
Zastolskiy Victor, Ran Zisovitch)

Library of Congress Cataloging-in-Publication Data
Murray, Laura K.
Tanks / Laura K. Murray.
p. cm. — (Seedlings)
Includes index.
Summary: A kindergarten-level introduction to tanks,
covering their drivers, weapons, role in battle, and such
defining features as their turrets.
ISBN 978-1-60818-665-5 (hardcover)
ISBN 978-1-62832-250-7 (pbk)
ISBN 978-1-56660-679-0 (eBook)
1. Tanks (Military science)—Juvenile literature. I. Title.

UG446.5.M86 2016
623.74'752—dc23   2015007566

CCSS: RI.K.1, 2, 3, 4, 5, 6, 7; RI.1.1,
2, 3, 4, 5, 6, 7; RF.K.1, 3; RF.1.1

First Edition HC 9 8 7 6 5 4 3 2 1
First Edition PBK 9 8 7 6 5 4 3 2 1

TABLE OF CONTENTS

Time to roll!

Tanks are heavy
machines with armor.

Militaries use
them in big fights.

The main part of a tank is called the hull. A large gun comes out of the turret.

Tracks help tanks move.

The tracks wrap around the wheels.

One person
drives the tank.
Three others sit
behind the driver.

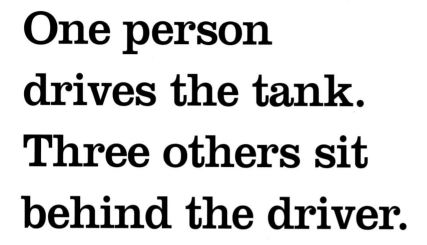

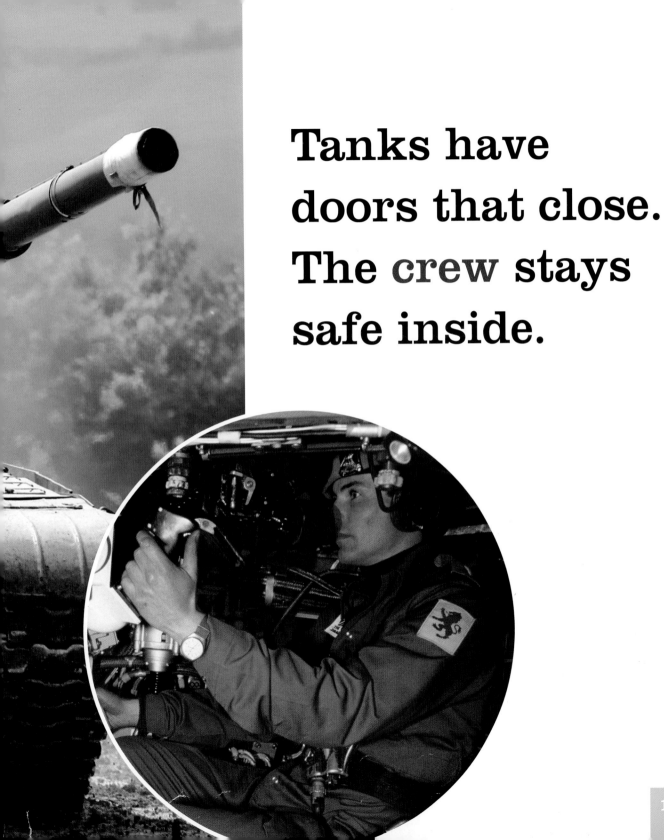

Tanks have doors that close. The **crew** stays safe inside.

A tank bumps over the ground. Its guns shoot.

Its armor
stays strong.

Go, tank, go!

Picture a Tank

gun

main gun

driver's hatch

light

track

hatch

interior

turret

hull

wheel

Words to Know

armor: a metal covering that keeps something safe

crew: a group of people who work on tanks

tracks: big, strong belts that go around a tank's wheels

turret: the tower on a tank that holds the main gun

Read More

Bozzo, Linda. *U.S. Army*.
Mankato, Minn.: Amicus, 2014.

Von Finn, Denny. *Abrams Tanks*.
Minneapolis: Bellwether Media, 2013.

Websites

Army Strong Videos
http://www.goarmy.com/army-videos.sch-Army%20Tanks
.html
Watch videos of U.S. Army tanks in action.

Military Coloring Pages
http://www.supercoloring.com/pages/category/military/
Print out a picture of an army tank to color.

Index